BIBLE WORD SEARCHES

D1307463

BARBOUR BOOKS
An Imprint of Barbour Publishing, Inc.

© 2001 by Barbour Publishing, Inc.

ISBN 1-57748-670-6

All rights reserved. No part of this publication may be reproduced or transmitted in any form or by any means without written permission of the publisher.

All Scripture references are from the King James Version of the Bible.

Published by Barbour Books, an imprint of Barbour Publishing, Inc., P.O. Box 719, Uhrichsville, Ohio 44683, www.barbourbooks.com

 Member of the
Evangelical Christian
Publishers Association

Printed in the United States of America.
5 4 3

BIBLE
WORD
SEARCHES

Pam Powell

Caught Up in a Whirlwind
(2 Kings 2:1-11)

BETHEL	LEAVE
CHARIOT	LIVETH
DIVIDED	LORD
DOUBLE	MANTLE
DRY	MASTER
ELIJAH	PORTION
ELISHA	PROPHETS
FIFTY	SMOTE
FIRE	SONS
GILGAL	SOUL
GROUND	SPIRIT
HARD	TWO
HEAD	VIEW
HEAVEN	WATERS
HORSES	WHIRLWIND
JERICHO	WRAPPED
JORDAN	

```
G F B H J E R I C H O H S E H
D I I J A O O S L O R D R E L
I P L F O R E J T W R I A V I
V O C G T R D L H E F D L I V
I R S D A Y D I I L H J K E E
D T L R A L R A D J E P F W T
E I U Y Z L T O N H A H O X H
D O O G W O U X H M E H T R L
I N S I I B C O A M G A A E P
O R N R L A R N S R A M V F B
W D A E H S T P O E E S A E L
T H E S E L I U T Y B V T T N
C K I S E R N O S O N S A E X
Z L D I I D M W A T E R S E R
E D E T H S W R A P P E D P L
```

Bonus Trivia

According to early church leader Tertullian (c. 200), why should men not shave?

Men who shave are saying they can make themselves look better than God did.

George Wayne Braun

Precious Things

AGATE
ALMUG
ALOES
AMETHYST
BERYL
BRASS
CARBUNCLE
CASSIA
CHALCEDONY
CHRYSOLITE
CHRYSOPRASE
CINNAMON
CONFECTION
CRYSTAL
DIAMOND
EMERALD

FRANKINCENSE
GOLD
JACINTH
JASPER
LIGURE
MYRRH
ONYX
PEARL
RUBY
SAPPHIRE
SARDIUS
SARDONYX
SILVER
SPICE
SPIKENARD
TOPAZ

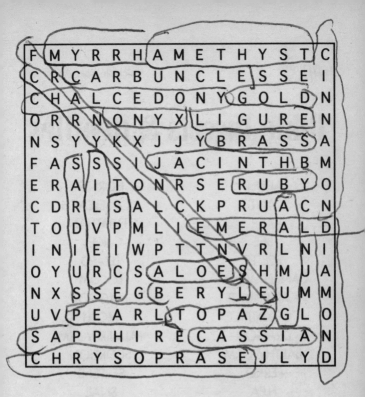

◇ Bonus Trivia

In His Steps is the best-selling religious novel in history. To the nearest $10,000, how much money did publishers have to give author Charles Sheldon for it?

$0 (He neglected to copyright it; some publishers voluntarily gave him money anyway.)

Michelle Ross Andersen

Bible Insects & Reptiles

ADDER

ANT

ASP

BEE

BEETLE

CANKERWORM

CATERPILLAR

COCKATRICE

DRAGON

EARTHWORM

FERRET

FLEA

FLY

FROG

GNAT

GRASSHOPPER

HORNET

HORSELEACH

LEVIATHAN

LICE

LIZARD

LOCUST

MAGGOT

MOTH

PALMERWORM

SCORPION

SERPENT

SNAIL

SPIDER

TORTOISE

VIPER

```
F M O F L Y L I Z A R D Q U M
G G M R O W H T R A E L F R O
E M R O W R E M L A P D D N L
R T N G Z M A L V I P E R O Y
C E Z E E S I O T R O T C G F
E R K O L P R M O T H U N A K
M R O W R E K N A C S C P R S
A E A E D E O T A T S I M D S
B F T I E I L E V I A T H A N
M A P F P O L T E N R O H Q A
C S E R P E N T E H G G B Z I
A R O S S T A D D E R G R P L
E C I R T A K C O C B A C Y D
S E O S F N G Y P I U M Y Z D
P H V K Q G A O L L R T E E B
```

◇ **Bonus Trivia**

Why did many churches quietly drop the second verse of "Jesus Loves the Little Children" in the 1970s?

It uses a term considered derogatory to the Japanese.

Michelle Ross Andersen

1 Corinthians 13

BEHAVE	MAN
CHARITY	MEN
CHILDISH THINGS	MYSTERIES
ENDURETH	NEVER FAILETH
ENVIETH NOT	NOT PUFFED UP
FACE TO FACE	REMOVE MOUNTAINS
FAITH	SOUNDING BRASS
GIFT OF PROPHECY	SUFFERETH LONG
GREATEST	THINKETH NO EVIL
HOPETH	THROUGH A GLASS
INIQUITY	TINKLING CYMBAL
KIND	TONGUES
KNOWLEDGE	TRUTH

```
S Y C E H P O R P F O T F I G
N C T D S T S E T A E R G H N
I J H N S E O F A I T H E T O
A M I I A S U H T U R T C E L
T I N K L I N G C Y M B A L H
N E K N G D D M N H E T F I T
U N E O A E I Y A O N Y O A E
O V T W H N N S C P T T T F R
M I H L G D G T H E B I E R E
E E N E U U B E A T E U C E F
V T O D O R R R R H H Q A V F
O H E G R E A I I N A I F E U
M N V E H T S E T A V N N N S
E O I U T H S S Y M E I F G G
R T L P U D E F F U P T O N S
```

◇ **Bonus Trivia**

Who said, "Within 100 years of my death, the Bible will be extinct"?

Voltaire.

Michelle Ross Andersen

Joyfulness

BREAK FORTH INTO

COUNT IT ALL JOY

EXCEEDING

FIELD

FULL

FULLNESS

HILLS

HOUSE

INCREASED

LEAPED

LIPS

MOTHER

NO GREATER JOY

NOISE

OF THE EARTH

OF THE LORD

OIL

REAP

SAINTS

SHOUT

SING

SOUL

SOUND

UNSPEAKABLE

VOICE

```
B R E A K F O R T H I N T O L
C F V O B S S R E S X Z L D U
N O G R E A T E R J O Y E N O
D N U G I F U L L N E S S R S
E X O N F J U T L E A P E D H
T B T I T H T R A E E H T F O
D S E D S I N G R A T S T F U
Z L G E E E T C K O P O T Q T
D C O E C H N A M I C H O J Y
V H W C Z I B Y L D E U I Y E
Y Y C X F L O H I L Q R F F F
W R R E E L A V O F J T S S T
S T V L O S D R V U V O S H N
X W Z U J A D N U O S B Y T W
Z P P X O T C I P P A E R Z V
```

Bonus Trivia

What is former president Carter's denominational affiliation?

Baptist.

D. Holm

Important Words in Ephesians

ALL	MYSTERY
AMEN	NIGH
APOSTLES	OBEY
ARMOUR	PAUL
BLESSINGS	PEACE
BODY	PLACES
CHILDREN	POWER
CHRIST	PROMISE
CHURCH	PUT OFF
EPHESIANS	SAINTS
EVANGELISTS	SAVED
FAITH	SEALED
FATHERS	SEE
FLESH	SIT
GOSPEL	SPIRIT
GRACE	STAND
HAVE	STRENGTHENED
HEAD	TEACHERS
HOLY	TOGETHER
JESUS	TRUTH
LOINS	WILES
MEN	WILL

N	R	R	E	W	O	P	R	O	M	I	S	E	F	M
E	E	V	A	N	G	E	L	I	S	T	S	Q	A	Y
P	H	R	H	E	A	D	T	T	R	U	T	H	I	S
H	T	C	D	L	U	A	P	E	A	C	E	N	T	T
E	E	H	H	L	O	I	N	S	A	M	E	N	H	E
S	G	R	I	N	I	G	H	U	C	C	I	J	C	R
I	O	I	F	A	T	H	E	R	S	A	H	A	B	Y
A	T	S	C	H	E	A	C	Y	S	O	R	E	A	T
N	H	T	E	U	E	V	L	E	B	G	J	B	R	I
S	G	N	I	S	S	E	L	B	O	D	E	V	A	S
M	E	N	T	E	P	T	A	O	D	Q	S	H	R	E
D	M	A	L	S	S	H	O	L	Y	D	U	S	M	A
W	N	I	O	O	C	H	U	R	C	H	S	E	O	L
D	W	G	P	U	T	O	F	F	W	I	L	L	U	E
P	L	A	C	E	S	P	I	R	I	T	L	F	R	D

◇ Bonus Trivia

What famous short work begins, "Lord, make me an instrument of thy peace"?

"The Prayer of Francis of Assisi."

D. Holm

42 Important Things in 1 Timothy

APOSTLE	JESUS
AUTHORITY	LAW
BEHAVIOUR	LEARN
BISHOP	LIFE
BOLDNESS	LORD
CHARGE	MEN
CHARITY	MINISTRY
DEACONS	ORDER
DOCTRINE	POWER
ELDERS	PRAYER
FABLES	PREACHER
FAITH	REPORT
GAIN	REWARD
GIFT	RICH
GLORY	RULE
GOD	SINS
GODLINESS	TRUST
GOOD WORKS	WIDOW
GOSPEL	WIVES
GRACE	WORDS
HONOUR	YOUTH

```
G O D L I N E S S Y O U T H B
O O W I V E S P M P R A Y E R
O S S D R O W R U O N O H K L
D R E P O R T S E L B A F I M
W D H R E W A R D V V R F Y R
O S Y R O L G P J I E E T F E
R T T U O F R D O D W I D O W
K G I L D E R U R S R H P W O
S R R E A O R O W O T H A D P
I A A C L T C N H I C L J E E
N C H A R G E T A I E T E A L
S E C U I M U F R A V F S C D
R F S B G A I N R I A I U O E
Q T Y R T S I N I M N G S N R
B P O H S I B O L D N E S S
```

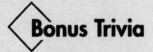

Bonus Trivia

What is the denominational affiliation of former president Richard Nixon?

Quaker.

Beth Umlauf

John the Baptist

BAPTIZED	LOCUSTS
BEHEADED	OATH
DAMSEL	PREACHING
ELISABETH	PREPARE YE THE WAY
HEROD	PRISON
HERODIAS	PROPHET
HONEY	REPENTANCE
JESUS	WILDERNESS
JORDAN RIVER	WITNESS
LAMB OF GOD	ZACHARIAS

```
P H E R O D I A S L G L T C D
R O B U R E V I R N A D R O J
E N Z Y G T N P V M S U A W I
P E Z M Y O I R B Z F T Z I S
A Y S T S U C O L L H E S L N
R T U I W T F P Z N Y C A D V
E T R Q A G T H Y M L N I E B
Y P G Z O L D E A B R A R R D
E D H D M O D T A N L T A N E
T J Y C R Z I Y E L F N H E Z
H H T E B A S I L E K E C S I
E E H Q O J E S U S T P A S T
W I T N E S S R V M V E Z I P
A W B W G N I H C A E R P Q A
Y T T R E J A D E D A E H E B
```

◇ Bonus Trivia

What book of the Bible furnished the lyrics for the Byrds' hit song "Turn, Turn, Turn"?

Ecclesiastes.

Twelves of the Bible

ANGELS	OXEN
APOSTLES	PATRIARCHS
BASKETS	PILLARS
BRETHREN	RODS
CAKES	SONS
CITIES	SPOONS
CUBITS	STARS
FOUNDATIONS	STONES
FOUNTAINS	THOUSAND
GATES	TRIBES
LEGIONS	WELLS
OFFICERS	YEARS

```
S R E C I F F O S R A E Y A X
K T L F N D O C L O P A N X S
R H C K L E U R L R O U E L R
S O V U V P N A E H S S R E A
Y U S E N O T S W K T C H G T
E S O I X R A N G E L S T I S
B A E E I E I O Q C E F E O H
G N N B T E N I C A S X R N C
E D E A F T S T E K S A B S R
P S K S G E G A T E S H K U A
A C S E Z I O D C S T U H Q I
R K V I G S C N U S Q X H Q R
R Q B T U I N U D C A M I L T
C U B I T S P O O N S F W P A
D U H C G U R F S R A L L I P
```

Bonus Trivia

What Christian leader said, "We shall match your capacity to inflict suffering with our capacity to endure suffering"?

Dr. Martin Luther King, Jr., about the white racists.

Karen Dickson

Praise!!

ADORE	OBEY
BLESS	OFFER
BREATHE	PERFECT
CONTINUALLY	SACRIFICE
EXALT	SEVEN TIMES
EXTOL	~~SHOUT~~
~~GIVE~~	SING
GLORIFY	SPEAK
HEAVEN AND EARTH	THANKSGIVING
HEIGHTS	WAIT
HONOR	WORKS
LEAP	WORTHY
LOVE	

```
S K R O W G I V E B V B G E G
D H C S E M I T N E V E S C K
P A E L N E Q S H V L Q I G X
Y L L A U N I T N O C D N N Y
W X B F V I A W T L A S G I K
S T H G I E H E X T O L I V S
E L F C R H N V E Q P N G I L
C Y E B O C T A I Y E A Y G I
I W O N F D R Y N C R Z Q S W
F V O E F E F W F D F B D K O
I R S A E I X A K A E P S N R
R Z S D R Z A A T A C A X A T
C U E O A G H Q L V T K R H H
A B L R E S H O U T F D S T Y
S G B E W A I T M W H Z Z T H
```

◇ **Bonus Trivia**

What country possesses the tallest church tower?

Germany (Cologne Cathedral, 512 feet).

Karen Dickson

Paul's Missionary Journeys

ANTIOCH	PAMPHYLIA
ATTALIA	PAPHOS
CILICIA	PERGA
CYPRUS	PHENICE
DERBE	PHILIPPI
EPHESUS	PISIDIA
GALATIA	ROME
ICONIUM	SAMARIA
LYCAONIA	SAMOTHRACIA
LYSTRA	SYRIA
MACEDONIA	THESSALONICA
MYSIA	TROAS
NEAPOLIS	

```
E S A O R T L G A L A T I A I
B P A P H O S R S B Z Q N I A
D E R B E W T S R A A T F C C
A G R E P S A M A R I A A A I
Q B C C Y P R U S O M I E R N
P H I L I P P I C W E R P H O
P I L A V I S H I M A Y H T L
A A I I Z S P H O P T S E O A
M I C S S I H R R F T D S M S
P N I Y C D E R R Q A A U A S
H O A M U I N O C I L L S S E
Y A D N Y A I Q I K I G O R H
L C R B Z B C Y E A A L W M T
I Y E B T T E N E A P O L I S
A L M A C E D O N I A N R M Y
```

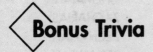

Bonus Trivia

Of the original thirteen colonies, how
many had Protestant origins?

12 (all but Maryland).

Carole Stengel

The Prophets

AARON	JEHU
AHIJAH	JEREMIAH
AMOS	JOEL
BALAAM	JONAH
DANIEL	MALACHI
DAVID	MEDAD
ELDAD	MICAH
ELIJAH	MOSES
ELISHA	NAHUM
EZEKIEL	NATHAN
GAD	OBADIAH
HABAKKUK	SAMUEL
HAGGAI	SHEMAIAH
HANANI	ZACHARIAS
HOSEA	ZECHARIAH
IDDO	ZEPHANIAH
ISAIAH	

```
H A I A S I B H A C I M G D H
M G N H A I M E R E J U N A A
V W D G A T A H I J A H B V I
S Z G G V J Y L E I N A D I N
B A K A E L I S H A K N E D A
H C E X J Z J R D K M W B M H
O H S A M U E L U H E J O O P
S A H I A O R K Q W D S O S E
E R E L V N H A I R A H C E Z
A I M A L A C H I E D I L S G
D A A G I T X A F H L D B N J
X S I D M H Q N Q E A I K O E
J E A D G A S O O D P W J R H
K B H A V N R J U I N A N A H
O D D I M A A L A B N L H A H
```

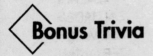

Bonus Trivia

In the thirteenth century, most laypeople
could not read, so what became known as
"the Scripture of the laity"?

Religious artwork.

Carole Stengel

Characteristics of Christ

ALIVE	HUMBLE
BENEVOLENT	JUST
COMPASSIONATE	LOVING
DISCERNING	MEEK
FAITHFUL	MERCIFUL
FORGIVING	POWER
GENTLE	RIGHTEOUS
GOOD	SERVES
GUILELESS	SINLESS
HARMLESS	SPOTLESS
HEALS	TEACHES
HELPING	TRUE
HOLY	WISE

```
G S E V R E S C B L G C S S Y
N S P F S Y F O R E U B I U J
I E G O M K I M Q J I N X O U
N L N R T V L P D B L O P E R
R M I G S L G A E E H R T R
E R P I U U E S S N L U R H E
C A L V J F N S K E E M W G W
S H E I V I T I S V S B F I O
I K H N S C L O U O S L S R P
D O O G E R E N O L P E M Q C
A W M S H E O A L E O H J P A
Y X K L C M H T A N U V V L Z
T L X A A O U E E T M R I M S
U J O E E L R O Z G H V T N S
L U F H T I A F G Q E N U C G
```

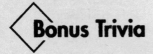

Bonus Trivia

What are catechumens?

People undergoing instruction for baptism.

Barbara Holt

Plagues of Egypt

AARON

BLOOD

BOILS

BONDAGE

BRICK

CATTLE

DARKNESS

DIE

DOORPOST

EGYPT

FIRE

FIRSTBORN

FLIES

FROGS

HAIL

LAMB

LICE

LOCUST

MAGICIANS

MIRACLE

MOSES

PHARAOH

PONDS

RIVER

ROD

SERPENT

SIGNS

STRAW

SWARMS

TASKMASTERS

THUNDER

WIND

WONDERS

```
T A S K M A S T E R S X L J S
H A I L T S O P R O O D O F M
U F X Q H K F U Z F X B C B R
N L K E C I L S T R A W U S A
D A K I O F E S B O I L S R W
E M R D S S W Q M G E I T T S
R B L O O D R B C S G G V H F
D O R M A G I C I A N S O I L
E N P G P E V Z A M L A R T I
L D N I W Y E G U T R S S N E
C A I M A E R I F A T E Y E S
A G O E G Y P T H B C L S P I
R E Q B K J Z P O N D S E R G
I N N F A C S R E D N O W E N
M X A A R O N D A R K N E S S
```

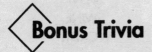

Bonus Trivia

Where was Christian traveling to in *The Pilgrim's Progress*?

Celestial City.

Barbara Holt

The Prodigal Son

ALIVE	HUSKS
CALF	JOURNEY
COMPASSION	KISSED
DANCING	LOST
DEAD	MERRY
EAT	MUSIC
ELDER	RING
FAMINE	ROBE
FATHER	SAFE
FEED	SERVANTS
FIELD	SHOES
FOUND	SON
GLAD	SPENT
HOUSE	SWINE
HUNGER	WORTHY

```
H S R O B E H U B Q S F I Y E
H K I S S E D Z Y G E N G N Q
V S N K I H I A Q R O L I A Y
D U G L P E V I L A H W A W H
J H O U S E P E H G S P E N T
Q S T D I J O U R N E Y T A R
T S A A D S N A O I R U N U O
G E S F E G G I T C V K R Q W
A L D A E D S L I N A G F W Y
Q C V R F S N S F A N A I R A
G D W N A L U T B D T H E N S
Y N S P M M A Z P H S D L Q W
Z U M I I E Y C E N L C D T S
X O U Y N X Y R R E M H M J O
C F O A E L E Z Z B M Y U W N
```

⬦ **Bonus Trivia**

What president wrote that he would like to see built "a wall of separation between church and state"?

Thomas Jefferson.

Ruth A. Graether

Bible Promises

"Casting all your _CARES_ upon him; for he careth for you" 1 Peter 5:7.

"I will never _leave_ thee, nor _forsake_ thee" Hebrews 13:5.

"The LORD is my _light_; I shall not _fear_" Psalm 23:1.

Commit thy way unto the _LORD_; _trust_ also in him; and he shall bring it to pass" Psalm 37:5.

"Be of good _cheer_ and he shall _str_ thine _strength_ Psalm 27:14.

"When thou _go_ through the _fire_, I will be with thee" Isaiah 43:2.

"When he shall _come Return_, we shall be like _him_; for we shall see him as he is" 1 John 3:2.

"Be not _dism_; for I am thy God" Isaiah 41:10.

"He giveth _____ to the _____; and to them that have no might he increaseth strength" Isaiah 40:29.

" _Jesus_ the same _Y_, and _T_, and _tomorr_ " Hebrews 13:8.

"My God shall _S_ all your _needs_ according to his _R_ in _C_ by Christ Jesus" Philippians 4:19.

"_Come_ unto me, and I will _S_ thee" Jeremiah 33:3.

"Thou wilt keep him in _P_ _P_, whose _mind_ is stayed on thee: because he trusteth in thee" Isaiah 26:3.

"God is my _R_; I will trust, and not be _D_ " Isaiah 12:2.

```
L W E C A E P T C E F R E P N
L J E S U S C H R I S T P C C
E K A S R O F A S Z Y U F F O
A H P C U S D E Y A M S I D M
V I C R M R T T D E E N Q Y M
E M A A I D D R E H P E H S I
V G L N N Z E E E E R L D F T
E R L S D T D F T N A W O O S
V A V W S I F V S S G C A R E
U E H E A A T R U S T T F E D
A P Y R I G V P O W E R H V W
V P F N D L P A S S E T H E W
P A T S A L V A T I O N F R N
T O D A Y R O L G S R E T A W
T R A E H V C C Y R I C H E S
```

◇ **Bonus Trivia**

At the end of the nineteenth century in
America, there was one Protestant church
per how many citizens?

450.

D. Holm

Job's Trials

AROSE	LORD
CHALDEANS	MORNING
CURSED	NAKED
DAUGHTERS	NONE
DEAD	OFFERED
DRINK	PERFECT
EARTH	PRESENCE
EAST	PRESENT
EATING	SABEANS
EVIL	SANCTIFIED
FACE	SATAN
FEAR	SERVANT
FELL	SINNED
FORTH	SONS
GOD	SUBSTANCE
GREATEST	SWORD
HAND	UPRIGHT
HEARTS	UZ
HEDGE	WALKING
HOUSES	WIND
JOB	WINE

```
U Z W I N E T C E F R E P E E
L P N R C U R S E D L R T A C
R I R L M M Q A O O E D D S N
S N S I V O R G R S E E N T E
O A N U G E R D E I N A N D S
F K T F B H V N F N E H R D E
F E N A I S T I I D F O A D R
E D A C N E T S L N W U Z N P
R E V E G C N A J S G S F I V
E A R D N A H O N H L E O W E
D D E A E C B W T C L S R A A
N H S B G G R E A T E S T M R
O C A H E A R T S M F I H K T
N S O N S S B D R I N K I N H
E X I W A L K I N G E S O R A
```

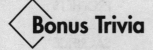

Bonus Trivia

According to a hymn, what is the only
way "to be happy in Jesus"?

Trust and obey.

The Contest: God & Baal
(1 Kings 18)

ABUNDANCE	HEART
AHAB	ISRAEL
ALOUD	JOURNEY
ALTAR	KNOWN
ANSWER	LORD
AWAKED	MANNER
BAAL	MOCKED
BARRELS	MORNING
BLOOD	NAME
BUILT	OFFERING
BULLOCK	PEOPLE
CHOOSE	PROPHETS
CONSUMED	RAIN
CRIED	SACRIFICE
CUT	SERVANT
DAY	SLEW
ELIJAH	STONES
FACES	TRENCH
FELL	VOICE
FIRE	WATER
HEAR	WOOD

```
M R B L O O D E I R C C U T N
O D E X U X R J A L O U D B N
R E C N O D O T B N A M E A E
N K W Z N U L P S A Y C K R C
I A A J R A Z U R A H D C R I
N W T N R I M Y D O B A O E F
G A E Y S E L P O E P Z M L I
B Y R R D W B S C V H H L S R
A H A F T U E N V S U E E I C
A E D R L N A R E F F R L T A
L A A L O D E C I O V A I J S
A E O T N K A R Y A R I J D L
H C S U B F E H N E Z N A O E
K C B U I L T T R E N C H O W
M A O F F E R I N G K N O W N
```

◇ Bonus Trivia

What nature song is known as "The Crusaders' Hymn"?

"Fairest Lord Jesus."

D. Holm

Hosea's Story

ADULTERIES	HUSBAND
ALLURE	ISRAEL
ANOTHER	JEZREEL
BACK	KING
BELOVED	LOAMMI
BOUGHT	LORD
BREAD	LORUHAMAH
CHILDREN	LOVERS
CONCEIVED	MOTHER
DAUGHTER	NAKED
DAYS	PEOPLE
DIBLAIM	RETURN
FIELD	SILVER
FIRST	VINEYARD
FRIEND	WALL
GOD	WHOREDOMS
GODS	WIFE
GOMER	WILL
HARLOT	WOMAN
HOSEA	

```
B P P I F I E L D E R U L L A
F E L A A V N F M A L A L O H
R O L L E R D O I E Y N K A B
I P I O U S T S E W E S R M G
E L W T V H O R V R S L I M O
N E E H E E Z H D E O A H I D
D R R R O E D L I T L A R A N
E F V E J R I R H B M A E F A
V I N T V H E G I A D R M N B
I R A H C T U D H S B P O K S
E S K G L O M U O L R T G I U
C T E U B D R O L M H A L N H
N E D A W O M A N E S V E G N
O A C D L O V E R S E W A L L
C K H V I N E Y A R D S D O G
```

◇ **Bonus Trivia**

In Nathaniel Hawthorne's *The Scarlet Letter*, what was the letter and what did it stand for?

A for Adultery.

Janice A. Buhl

Crucifixion

BARABBAS	JUDAS ISCARIOT
BETHANY	KING
BETRAYED	KISS
BLASPHEMY	MOUNT OF OLIVES
BLOOD	PASSOVER
BODY	PONTIUS PILATE
CAIAPHAS	PRAY
CROWN	PRIESTS
CRUCIFIED	SCRIBES
CUP	SILVER
DISCIPLES	SOLDIERS
ELDERS	THIRTY PIECES
GETHSEMANE	UNLEAVENED

```
M G C U P D G P B S N K V T Y
O X Y T O A R S C E I W H I D
U E E O O I S R R S T I O T O
N N L T E E I S S E R H O R B
T B L S A B N A O T I I A L C
O C T E E L H A Y V R D A N H
F S D S A P I P M A E S L S Y
O S Z E A V I P C E P R E O D
L C A I I E E S S H S L D E S
I E A B C F I N E U P H Y G R
V C L E B S I M E I I A T E B
E K S D A A Y C C D R T V E K
S S Y D E A R S U T C L N I G
D E U O R R I A E R I Q N O F
U J X P C D S B B S C G C R P
```

◇ Bonus Trivia

"Jesus, the very thought of Thee/With sweetness fills my breast." But according to that hymn, what is even sweeter?

Jesus' face.

Janice A. Buhl

Ruth

BARLEY

BETHLEHEM

BLESSED

BOAZ

CHILION

DAUGHTERS-IN-LAW

DIED

ELIMELECH

FAMINE

FAVOR

GLEAN

JUDAH

KINSMAN

LOVE

MAHLON

MAIDENS

MARA

MOAB

NAOMI

OBED

ORPAH

RUTH

SONS

VIRTUOUS

WIFE

WIVES

```
D F H A M F N Y G B O A Z F G
C A F C A A N A L Q Q I V P L
M J U M E O I E M A H L O N E
K E I G I L S D B S F P L Y A
S N H L H S E A E Y N D F E N
E U I E E T R M Y N L I R W C
H H O D L L E E I E S E K I S
C G J U E H G R J L S D M B E
R F W Y T E T P S G E N E U V
N P C E Y R D E U I W T I J I
H U F C J Z I X B V N W M E W
A R A M I H I V Y I S L O F M
D P V K T F H A P R O E A I E
U E O U Y W J Y W V N D N W C
J X R Z H I O B E D S B A O M
```

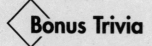

Bonus Trivia

What letter did Martin Luther call "my epistle, to which I am betrothed"?

Galatians.

Janice A. Buhl

"S" Names

SADDUCEES

SAMARITAN

SAMSON

SAMUEL

SAPPHIRA

SARAH

SATAN

SELAH

SETH

SHAHAR

SHALLUM

SHAPHAT

SHARON

SHAUL

SHEBA

SHECHEM

SHELAH

SHILOH

SHIMEA

SHUR

SILVANUS

SIMEON

SIMON

SODOM

SOLOMON

STEPHEN

SYRIA

```
S H U R N S X Z S S H I M E A
Z L V A H K X K H T Z A S B R
A E T A A H L A N B E H L L I
R A R N A I H A A O A P E E R
S O S L A A R M R P M U H W S
N L E U R T U Y H I M O X E M
V H N S N L I A S A H C L S N
S W E O L A T R S N L P E O S
Y T M A M N V T A W H E P A S
H P H E O I U L M M C P M A H
I S X E H Y S Z I U A S Q O S
F A M I T C T C D S O S L A W
K I Z A T Z E D H N E I R Z Q
S O D O M U A H O C H A A V C
S A B E H S M O S S H A U L S
```

◇ **Bonus Trivia**

Which president signed the bill to add the words "under God" to the Pledge of Allegiance?

Dwight Eisenhower.

Janice A. Buhl

"M" Names

MACEDONIA	MERARI
MACHI	MERCURIUS
MANASSEH	MESHACH
MANOAH	MESOPOTAMIA
MARA	MICAH
MARANATHA	MICHAEL
MARK	MIDIAN
MARTHA	MIRIAM
MARY	MIZPAH
MATHUSALA	MOAB
MATTHEW	MORDECAI
MEDIA	MORIAH
MELCHISEDEC	MOSES
MEMPHIS	MYRA

```
A X M Y F H A C I M I D I A N
H B K E A K H T E W I M Y L R
T V F P R C U M F J X R A V P
R V Z R A C P H U S W K I R M
A I D H C H U K E E T A M A K
M A S M I E O R H S I A R A M
F E I S O H D T I M S A I A A
M L Y N A R T E A U N A L Z C
A H E O O A D T S A S A N Z H
R I N A M D O E T I S L H A I
Y A R C H P E H C U H A M M M
M E J A O C A C H A I C E L B
Y U N S R C I T A R I D L G A
R V E L J E A M O M I B A E O
A M A G Z M M M F A S E S O M
```

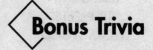

Bonus Trivia

Who said at his martyrdom that he had served Christ for eighty-six years?

Polycarp.

Revelation

ALPHA
ANGEL
BEASTS
BLOOD
BOOK
CANDLESTICKS
CHURCHES
DRAGON
ELDERS
FIRE
GATES
HORSES
JOHN
LAKE OF FIRE
LAMB

LION
OMEGA
PATMOS
PROPHECY
SEALS
SEATS
STARS
SWORD
TESTIMONY
THOUSAND
THRONE
TRIBES
TRIBULATION
TRUMPETS
WORMWOOD

```
Z T R I B E S S Q T S L A E S
G B M A L G T U H E E N H O J
A B B D P S Z R U G D F V N Z
T Y E S A D O U N F I O R V T
E R L E K N T A H R A W O R N
S V B O E C Z E E P E G I L P
N O G A R D I Y S R A B E B B
S E A T S D C T I T U T S M C
H T L W H E O F S L I T M H O
K O O F H O F O A E E M U O S
H R R P A O U T W P L R O T S
D Y O S E H I S M M C D A N B
Y R T K E O P U A H R R N O Y
P S A Q N S R L E N S O O A Q
T L I O N T Q S A X D K W P C
```

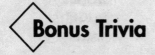

Bonus Trivia

What American colony was founded as a refuge for Quakers?

Pennsylvania.

Janice A. Buhl

David and Goliath

ABINADAB	JUDAH
AFRAID	KILL
ARMIES	MAIL
BATTLE	MOUNTAIN
BRASS	PHILISTINES
DAVID	SAUL
ELIAB	SERVANTS
FIGHT	SHAMMAH
FOREHEAD	SHIELD
GATH	SHOCHO
GOLIATH	SLING
GREAVES	SPEAR
HEIGHT	STONES
HELMET	TARGET
ISRAEL	VALLEY

```
F O R E H E A D T O S Y B V G
I M Q U Y D P A Z E H A A O Q
G S A U L E R E R S T C L Z M
H Q E E Y G L V F T E I O O M
T M I N E Q A L L N A I U H T
T H L T I N K E A T R N M I S
S E L U T T S B H V T A R R S
T L I S I E S M A A B I E H A
O I K K V L O I I D S R A P D
N A S A I T T N L R A M A D S
E B E N E H O H A I M N I S D
S R G M G H M E A A H A I A S
G C L I T J L A H D R P V B I
J E E A B R G F I F U I R M A
H H G A A A W L A L D J E K B
```

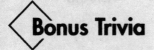

Bonus Trivia

What snack food was supposedly invented
by a seventh-century Italian monk to
reward children who memorized prayers?

Pretzels.

Judy Ellis

Day of...

ADVERSITY	INDIGNATION
AFFLICTION	JERUSALEM
ATONEMENT	JEZREEL
BATTLE	JUDGMENT
CHRIST	MIDIAN
CLOUDS	PENTECOST
DARKNESS	RAIN
DEATH	REDEMPTION
DISTRESS	SLAUGHTER
EGYPT	TEMPTATION
EVIL	TROUBLE
GOD	VENGEANCE
GRIEF	VISITATION

```
B A T T L E S S O L F X L S E
R F N S E E Y S H C D E M S M
B F E O N M C C E J H E I E A
V L M C O E P Z L N O R A R A
D I G E A L A T G O K T I T G
R C D T R A D Y A I U R R S H
E T U N E S V T T G D A I T
D I J E T U E E O A I V S D R
E O W P H R R I N N T O F J O
M N X J G E S Z E G A P N D U
P U I P U J I W M I E I Y O B
T D Y R A T T J E D D A D G L
I E F Q L X Y L N N M W N I E
O J V I S I T A T I O N B C M
N I A R W J E Z R E E L I V E
```

Bonus Trivia

What biblical region is fittingly mentioned in the hymn "Send the Light"?

Macedonia.

Judy Ellis

Weapons

ARMOUR	HOOKS
ARROWS	KNIFE
AX	PLOWSHARES
BOW	PRUNINGHOOKS
BUCKLERS	QUIVER
BURN	SHIELDS
CAPTIVITY	SLINGS
DART	SPEARS
FLAME	SPOIL
HABERGEON	STONES
HANDSTAVES	SWORD
HELMETS	TORCHES

```
C S T O N E S T R A D A S S U
A G A Q X N Q U I V E R W T D
P N R Z R O T G H K E Y O D T
T I E U U E Z L G L T H R W Z
I L B Q O G N V K F M Q R A S
V S S P M R T C E S M H A S H
I K G D R E U O E L E A X L I
T O J O A B Y R Q L K N I F E
Y O N J O A A O M V N D W P L
W H R W B H P E I S H S S U D
T V R C S Y T J T E R T S L S
Q N C W H S R U H O F A A I U
C P O B R E F Y L I K V E O Z
H L K B Z Y S F L A M E W P P
P R U N I N G H O O K S P S S
```

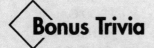

Bonus Trivia

What percentage of Christians shop at
Christian bookstores?

30 percent.

Evelyn M. Boyington

People Whose Prayers Are in the Bible

ABRAHAM	JEREMIAH
APOSTLES	JOB
BLIND	JOEL
DANIEL	JOHN
DAVID	JOSHUA
DISCIPLES	MANIAC
ELIJAH	MARTHA
ELISHA	MARY
EZRA	MOSES
GIDEON	PAUL
HANNAH	PETER
ISAAC	PRODIGAL
ISRAEL	RICH MAN
JABEZ	SAMSON
JACOB	SOLOMON
JAIRUS	STEPHEN

```
S L N X D T S A P L R U F D A
Y E S M C T J R L E A R S I W
U O L H E P O Z Q M T G L C I
N J C P A D A E J A B E Z Y Z
W G H A I N F H A H D C R H P
D E I G I C N H T A I A D A O
N M A D S N S A N R M T V J R
I L O D E I A I H B A J W I Y
L R V Y L O E M D A O M C L D
B Y U E T L N E B H D H J E B
P S A M S O N R N O M O L O S
A U H S O J R E X A R O C E R
U V L A P P I J N C A A S I H
L A Q P A S U R I A J O B E W
B C A N D Y J Q F Q A V J Y S
```

⟨ **Bonus Trivia**

What is often considered to be the oldest known Christian writing outside the New Testament, dating to perhaps A.D. 90?

I Clement.

Evelyn M. Boyington

Biblical Household Items

BAKING	PARLOUR
BED	PILLOW
CAKE	PITCHER
CANDLE	POST
CRUSE	POT
CUP	POTTAGE
DISH	SEWING
FIRE	SHOVEL
GREASE	SNUFFER
LAMP	SOAP
MEAL	SPICE
MIRROR	SPOON
MYRRH	TABLE
NITRE	VESSEL
OIL	WASH
PAN	WINE

L	F	Z	E	W	E	E	U	L	F	X	V	W	H	R
F	E	F	A	R	R	G	S	O	A	P	T	U	R	F
R	M	S	V	N	T	G	P	U	C	A	B	E	V	E
C	H	W	S	O	R	I	M	O	R	N	H	G	K	Q
R	S	P	G	E	L	D	N	A	C	C	L	A	M	P
R	I	U	A	A	V	W	A	S	T	E	C	T	S	T
C	D	S	N	R	P	J	P	I	F	O	A	T	W	G
Z	E	W	O	L	L	I	P	D	E	B	M	O	T	K
J	F	Z	O	L	C	O	H	C	L	I	O	P	J	F
B	L	K	P	E	E	S	U	E	R	N	Y	B	B	C
W	A	C	S	H	E	V	T	R	E	F	F	U	N	S
E	E	K	N	W	R	M	O	D	P	K	I	I	W	X
J	M	C	I	I	S	R	P	H	O	L	B	Y	R	Q
D	X	N	J	N	K	K	Y	H	S	T	G	Z	F	E
Q	G	Y	P	E	G	L	F	M	T	S	P	O	G	N

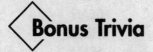

Bonus Trivia

According to the hymn, what will occur if you "count your many blessings"?

Angels will come to comfort you.

Evelyn M. Boyington

Measurements, Weights, and Money

BATH	LOG
BEKAH	MANEH
BUSHEL	MEASURE
CAB	MILE
COR	MINA
CUBIT	MITE
DARIC	OMER
DENARIUS	PACE
DIDRACHMA	POUND
DRACHMA	QUADRANS
EPHAH	REED
FARTHING	SEAH
FATHOM	SHEKEL
FIRKIN	SPAN
FURLONG	STATER
HOMER	TALENT

```
B C T D W X G C A K P N W S D
A F I R K I N Q L Z S E L I M
R M S R T A L E N T L S D Q W
M Q H N A G M E A S U R E W C
U C E C P D N T P S A C N F B
G R K S A R E I S C Y U A U D
I C E T C R L E H S U B R F Q
Y A L M E G D M R T E I I Q E
H A F M O F A X O K R T U M S
Y I O U A H E N A M E A S Q V
U F P T R H A H P E D W F Z V
M E H Q B L R Z L R A N I M V
T O T C W X O R A T N X U G S
M J A I L L C N N H Z P C O R
E B B I M H S P G J K V I L P
```

⟨ **Bonus Trivia**

Why were love feasts forbidden by the church in the fourth century?

People were overeating and feeling stuffed all afternoon (some have noted a resemblance to contemporary pot luck dinners here).

Saul's Conversion

SAUL

THREATENING

SLAUGHTER

LETTERS

HIGH PRIEST

JOURNEYED

DAMASCUS

LIGHT

HEAVEN

FELL

WHY PERSECUTEST

THOU ME

JESUS

KICK AGAINST

THE PRICKS

TREMBLING

ASTONISHED

ARISE

SPEECHLESS

MEN

LED HIM

THREE

DAYS

DISCIPLE

ANANIAS

JUDAS

HOUSE

PRAY

VISION

SIGHT

BAPTIZED

```
W T D A M A S C U S X E N R G
H H A N A N I A S L L Y S N A
I G Y Z E B B E U P A L I T S
G I V P U M L A I R A N H M T
H L U S E H S C P U E G X D O
P T T R C R S R G T I W E A N
R H R E D I S H A S I Y L Y I
I E E T D X T E Z N E Z L S S
E P M T I E R A C N E H E M H
S R B E R H R S R U O V F D E
T I L L T I A U A U T I A S D
C C I R S D O S S A D E S E A
O K N E U J L E D H I M S I H
V S G J N N X J E M U O H T V
E E R H T S N I A G A K C I K
```

◇ **Bonus Trivia**

What was the date of the first complete
New Testament canon (list of books) as we
have it today?

A.D. 367.

Marcella Laverman

Philip's Calling

PHILIP	QUESTIONS
DISCIPLE	PROPHECY
CHOSEN	MESSIAH
PREACHER	SALVATION
SENT	EXPLAIN
GAZA	ACCEPTANCE
ETHIOPIAN	WATER
CHARIOT	BAPTISM
HORSES	HOLY SPIRIT
DESERT	CAUGHT AWAY
SCROLL	JOY
ISAIAH	NEW LIFE

```
Y C E H P O R P R E A C H E R
A Q O R I I Z N G P F G J X F
C H A I S S E M N E W L I F E
C T Q W T S Q C O E H J M I G
E R A N O N N A I P O I H T E
P E E H T F Z H T Y O D O V X
T S C R O L L B A P T I S M P
A E W I I B P W V E A L H X L
N D A N R K A D L E K Y H Q A
C Q T J A T D R A E Q V A P I
E T E F H O L Y S P I R I T N
I J R G C I V Y X I V L A N A
E Q U E S T I O N S I V S D Z
S A I G S E S R O H S L I Z A
C P E D I S C I P L E I N L G
```

Bonus Trivia

The religious poem (and song) "The Touch of the Master's Hand" compares our lives before Christ to what?

An old musical instrument.

Richard Hammer

Women of the Old Testament

ABIGAIL	KETURAH
BILHAH	LEAH
DEBORAH	MICHAL
DELILAH	MIRIAM
DINAH	NAOMI
ELISHEBA	ORPAH
ESTHER	RACHEL
EVE	RAHAB
HAGAR	REBEKAH
HEPHZIBAH	RUTH
HULDAH	SARAH
JEZEBEL	TAMAR
JOCHEBED	ZIPPORAH
JUDITH	

```
H A P R O V U V B A N Y H N F
K Q N A E C W B R A F J A Q H
W H V M X H A R O B E D D H A
N A C A A M T M M Z E E V E R
I E E T I B I S E B O L L V O
X X W R P C A B E U W I M M P
J V I U H I E H H G S L A X P
L A L A E L C A A H W A B N I
M W L E H O G W E R A H H R Z
D B H G J A H B L J U R U E K
F S I U R U A L O I Q T Z B R
W A Q L T L D I N A H O E E J
G R A C H E L I A G I B A K I
M A H S L A U G T H U H H A M
B H A B I Z H P E H Y O Q H Y
```

◇ **Bonus Trivia**

One of the great religious works of all time is Blaise Pascal's *Pensees*. What is its title in English?

Thoughts.

Sheryl J. Johnson

A Time to...
(Ecclesiastes 3:1-8)*

To every thing there is a <u>season</u>, and a time for every
 purpose under the <u>heaven</u>:
A time to be <u>born</u>,
 And a time to <u>die</u>;
A time to <u>plant</u>,
 And a time to <u>pluck</u> that which is planted;
A time to <u>kill</u>,
 And a time to <u>heal</u>;
A time to break <u>down</u>,
 And a time to <u>build</u> up;
A time to <u>weep</u>,
 And a time to <u>laugh</u>; ·
A time to <u>mourn</u>,
 And a time to <u>dance</u>;
A time to cast away <u>stones</u>,
 And a time to <u>gather</u> stones;
A time to <u>embrace</u>,
 And a time to <u>refrain</u> from embracing;
A time to <u>gain</u>,
 A time to <u>lose</u>;
A time to <u>keep</u>,
 And a time to <u>cast</u> away;
A time to <u>rend</u>,
 And a time to <u>sew</u>;
A time to keep <u>silence</u>,
 And a time to <u>speak</u>;

```
D N O S A E S I D N V E T A H
E C N E L I S A T N A L P N O
Q A V E C N A D V M E C A E P
I L B R H G B Q N I A R F E R
V A O Q Y E N E V A E H W O A
P E E W I S R V T U I A B H W
E H X E M O P A M K D L V G B
E V W S C L L I K X O U I U Y
K V X H U V R S C V R N I A G
K R E C A R B M E Q Y L U L R
N L K Y K N N N U F D G R K E
I R W B E A H I R X S K E N H
K R U T P B E N W O D C N T T
S E N O T S R P R P B Y D D A
Y F X K M R P R S C A S T K G
```

A time to <u>love</u>,
    And a time to <u>hate</u>;
A time of <u>war</u>,
    And a time of <u>peace</u>.

*Find only those words that are underlined.

Carol Wenzel

Adam to Jesus

ABIUD	JESUS
ABRAHAM	JUDAH
ADAM	KENAN
AHAZ	LAMECH
AKIM	MAHALEL
AMMINADAB	METHUSELAH
AMON	NAHOR
ARPHAZAD	NAHSHON
ASA	NOAH
AZOR	OBED
BOAZ	PELEG
DAVID	PEREZ
EBER	RAM
ELEAZAR	REU
ELIAKIM	SALMON
ELIUD	SERUG
ENOCH	SETH
ENOSH	SHELAH
ISAAC	SHEM
JACOB	SOLOMON
JARED	TERAH
JESSE	ZADOK

```
A N B H A L E S U H T E M C S
M B O A R D N K U C R M R E U
O N A R P E R E Z O Q A T N K
N O Z E H E J L Z N M H A O N
U H D T A M L A D E R A J S A
N S U C Z W J E S S E L Z H H
B H I J A C O B G U R E S D O
A A B U D P R A Z A E L E B R
D N A D D A S A L M O N E G N
A C K A M H C H X Z A D O K O
N E E H E A J J E S U S I M M
I P N M B Z D U I L E A S A O
M L A M E C H D I V A D A I L
M D N H R Z S A B R A H A M O
A K I M I K A I L E A X C L S
```

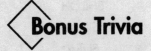

Bonus Trivia

For what offense was John Bunyan
(author of *The Pilgrim's Progress*) given a
twelve-year jail term?

Preaching without a license.

Carol Wenzel

Biblical Geography

ANTIOCH	MALTA
ARARAT	MOAB
ASSYRIA	NAIN
BABYLON	NAZARETH
BEREA	NILE
BETHANY	NINEVEH
BETHLEHEM	PATMOS
BETHSAIDA	PHILISTA
CANA	ROME
DAMASCUS	SAMARIA
DERBE	SHECHEM
EDOM	SHILOH
EGYPT	SINAI
GALILEE	SUSA
GETHSEMANE	TARSUS
GILGAL	TROAS
JERICHO	TYRE
JERUSALEM	UR
JOPPA	ZOAR
JORDAN	

```
D A M A S C U S O M T A P Y X
A R E A H P A T L A M E H A P
P A H E V E N I N E O N I L E
P R E E J W T O L L A G L I G
O A L I R P L A P J B I I O E
J T H G Y Y S H O L I H S A T
S R T G B U T B E R E A T D H
H O E A R H C O I T N A A I S
E A B E T H A N Y Y R D B A E
C S J E R I C H O S E N I S M
H A D O Z O A R U R A A R H A
E O N L R N M S B S N I U T N
M S M A B D F E U I B N U E E
S A M A R I A S S Y R I A B N
E E L I L A G N A Z A R E T H
```

Bonus Trivia

On what American monument can one find the Old Testament quote, "Proclaim liberty throughout all the land unto all the inhabitants thereof"?

The Liberty Bell.

Pamela Jensen

Waters

ABUNDANCE	JORDAN
ARNON	KANAH
CHINNERETH	KISHON
CILICIA	LAKES
CISTERN	LIVING
COLD	MARAH
DEAD	MEDITERRANEAN
DEEP	MIGHTY
EUPHRATES	NILE
FIRE	ORONTES
FOUNTAINS	OVERFLOWING
GAD	RED
GALILEE	RIVERS
GENNESARET	SALT
GIHON	SEAS
GREAT	STILL
JABBOK	STREAMS
JAZER	WELL
JOPPA	WIDE

```
L A K E S R E V I R G R E A T
S T R E A M S T I L L L L E W
A W A Y D B C J N O H I G L I
B S Q F C A F O S H A U G I D
U M E D I T E R R A N E A N E
N I U E S R V D A G L J L O J
D G P E T O E A N P T T I H A
A H H P E R G N I V I L L S B
N T R O R C I L I C I A E I B
C Y A S N I A T N U O F E K O
E T T O R O N T E S Z L C F K
Z G E N N E S A R E T S D T A
U L S O V E R F L O W I N G N
C H I N N E R E T H N O N R A
A P P O J A Z E R K M A R A H
```

◇ Bonus Trivia

What American President died the same day as C. S. Lewis?

John Kennedy.

Pamela Jensen

Prayer Themes

ADORATION	LONGING
ASK	LOVE
BLESSING	NO
BREAD	PETITION
CARE	POWER
CLEANSING	PRAISE
CONFESSION	PROTECTION
FASTING	RESTORATION
FELLOWSHIP	SONG
FORGIVENESS	SUBMISSION
FREE	THANKSGIVING
GLORY	TRUST
GUIDANCE	VISION
HEALING	VOW
HEAR	WAIT
HELP	WISDOM
INTERCESSION	WORD
JOY	YES
LIFE	

```
I N T E R C E S S I O N G P L
G N H G E O W I S D O M E B O
N O A N S N F A Y I R T C R N
O I N I T F A S I A I A N E G
S T K S O E S K E T R H A A I
S C S N R S T H I E G O D D N
E E G A A S I O H E A L I N G
N T I E T I N F N R X G U T N
E O V L I O G L I F E D G R I
V R I C O N O I S S I M B U S
I P N S N O I T A R O D A S S
G I G J I V Y D D H S A M T E
R E W O P V N R N E J E V O L
O O I Y N O O E G L O R Y U B
F E L L O W S H I P R A I S E
```

Bonus Trivia

What important Christian book contains the characters Slubgob, Wormwood, and Glubose?

The Screwtape Letters, by C. S. Lewis.

Pamela Jensen

Feasts

ATONEMENT	OFFERING
BLOOD	PASSOVER
BREAD	PENITENCE
CELEBRATE	PENTECOST
DELIVERANCE	PROMISED
EGYPT	PURIM
ESTHER	SABBATH
EXODUS	SACRIFICE
HAMAN	SOLEMN
HARVEST	TABERNACLES
HOLY	TEMPLE
LAND	TRUMPETS
LIGHTS	UNLEAVENED
MEMORIAL	WEEKS
MOON	WHEAT
MOURNING	WORSHIP
NEW	

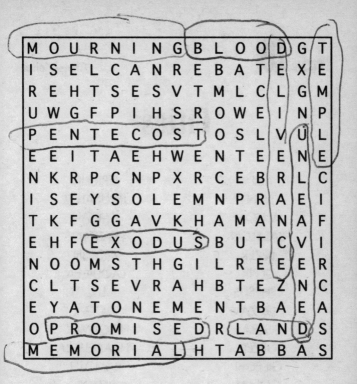

```
M O U R N I N G B L O O D G T
I S E L C A N R E B A T E X E
R E H T S E S V T M L C L G M
U W G F P I H S R O W E I N P
P E N T E C O S T O S L V U L
E E I T A E H W E N T E E N E
N K R P C N P X R C E B R L C
I S E Y S O L E M N P R A E I
T K F G G A V K H A M A N A F
E H F E X O D U S B U T C V I
N O O M S T H G I L R E E E R
C L T S E V R A H B T E Z N C
E Y A T O N E M E N T B A E A
O P R O M I S E D R L A N D S
M E M O R I A L H T A B B A S
```

Bonus Trivia

What document says people are "endowed by their Creator with certain unalienable Rights"?

The Declaration of Independence.

Cheryl Keiser

Cities

AI	JERICHO
AIN	JERUSALEM
ALMON	KARTAH
BABYLON	KARTAN
BEZER	KEDESH
DEBIR	LAODICEA
EPHESUS	LUZ
GAZA	OG
GEBA	PERGAMOS
GEZER	PHILADELPHIA
GIBEON	RAMOTH
GOLAN	REHOB
HEBRON	ROME
HOLON	SAMARIA
HORAN	SMYRNA
JATTIR	

```
Q U N A T R A K A R T A H P B
S U S E H P E E I M A X J E G
T R I B E D Y D N V L M Z R E
G A Z A E Q R E N A A E E G Z
E I S C O O K S I H R H F A E
B R M O M B D H J B O O A M R
A A I E H G A M Y B G L H O A
N M A W L N R B U T M P O S E
R A Z P O A R D Y O E H I N C
Y S L E M N S I N L C S S J I
M K B O Y O Q U T I O M X I D
S I T G G R Z D R T Y N S M O
G H Z O Q B X E F E A Z I Z A
I Y X B B E J W G M J J U R L
Z D V A I H P L E D A L I H P
```

◇ **Bonus Trivia**

What daughter of a famous pastor was
described by Lincoln as "the little lady
who made this big war"?

Harriet Beecher Stowe.

Carol Borror Leath

Noah's Great-Grandsons

ANAMIM	NAPHTUHIM
ASHKENAZ	NIMROD
CAPHTORIM	PATHRUSIM
CASLUHIM	RAAMAH
DODANIM	RIPHATH
ELISHAH	SABTAH
GETHER	SABTECHAH
HAVILAH	SALAH
HETH	SEBA
HUL	SIDON
KITTIM	TARSHISH
LEHABIM	TOGARMAH
LUDIM	UZ
MASH	

```
J G H E L I S H A H I P S C C
D J A G S Y M I S U R H T A P
H O M H E A P V E P Y C P S M
A H R P B T R A A M A H M L B
L Z A M A O H H C P T E I U Y
A T G L I R F E C O M T M H M
S X O D T N M K R E N H A I I
A L T A R S H I S H B A N M B
S I I U O F M H H H R A A G A
H M B V B K G A T U D K G Q H
K I T T I M V T D O T B I L E
E D N O D I S B D I H H U R L
N U X U L P O A H T A H P I R
A L M A S H R S Y L G R U A D
Z U H U Q S A B T E C H A H N
```

⬦ Bonus Trivia

The refrain of a Fanny Crosby hymn ends with "Let us hope and trust, Let us watch and pray, And labor till the Master comes." What is the first part of that refrain?

"Toiling on, toiling on, toiling on, toiling on, toiling on, toiling on, toiling on, toiling on."

Carol Borror Leath

Tabitha Raised to Life

ALMSDEEDS

DIED

DISCIPLE

DORCAS

FULL OF GOOD WORKS

GARMENTS

GAVE HIS HAND

JOPPA

KNEELED

KNOWN THROUGHOUT

LIFTED HER UP

LYDDA

OPENED HER EYES

PETER

PRAYED

PRESENTED ALIVE

SAINTS

SENT TWO MEN

SHE SAT UP

SHE WAS SICK

SHEWING THE COATS

"TABITHA, ARISE"

UPPER CHAMBER

WEEPING

WIDOWS

```
F T C P U R E H D E T F I L S
P U P P E R C H A M B E R G T
R O L S T N E M R A G G H A A
E H P L S A I N T S T N B V O
S G A L O P E T E R A I D E C
E U L D Y F U L C P T P E H E
N O M E W D G T P H R E Y I H
T R S L I J D O A I S E A S T
E H D E D B J A O S C W R H G
D T E E O Q R G A D E S P A N
A N E N W I D I E D W H I N I
L W D K S A C R O D K O S D W
I O S E N T T W O M E N R N E
V N N K C I S S A W E H S K H
E K O P E N E D H E R E Y E S
```

◇ Bonus Trivia

Approximately how many sermons did John Wesley preach?

40,000 (to better appreciate this feat, note that if a man preached fifteen sermons a week every week for fifty years, he would still come up short of Wesley's figure).

Word Search Answers

Puzzle #1

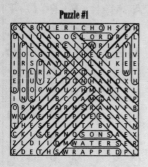

Puzzle #2

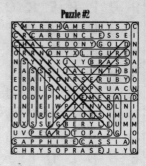

Puzzle #3

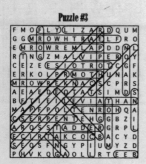

Puzzle #4

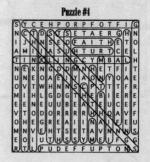

Puzzle #5

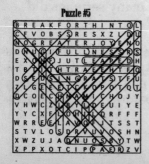

Puzzle #6

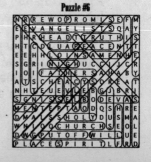

Puzzle #7

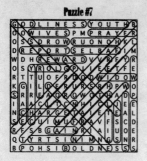

Puzzle #8

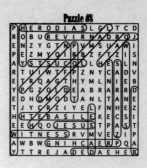

Puzzle #9

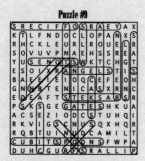

Puzzle #10

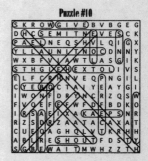

Puzzle #11

Puzzle #12

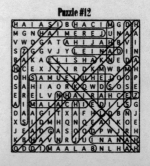

Puzzle #13

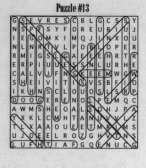

Puzzle #14

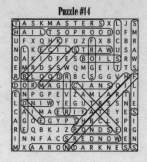

Puzzle #15

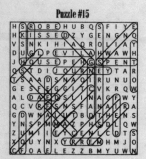

Puzzle #16

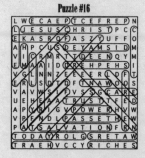

Puzzle #17

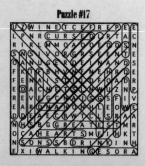

Puzzle #18

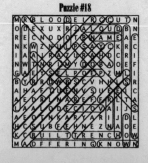

Puzzle #19

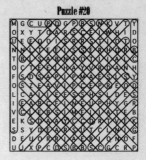

Puzzle #20

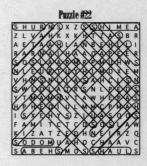

Puzzle #21

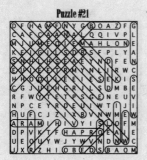

Puzzle #22

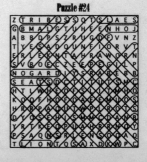

Puzzle #23

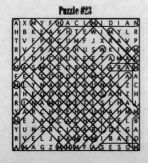

Puzzle #24

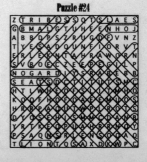

Puzzle #25

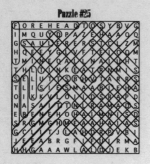

Puzzle #26

Puzzle #27

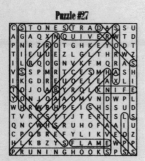

Puzzle #28

Puzzle #29

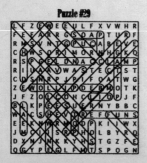

Puzzle #30

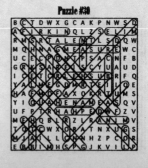

Puzzle #31

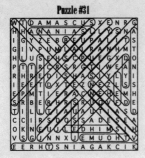

Puzzle #32

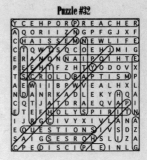

Puzzle #33

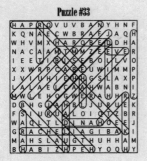

Puzzle #34

Puzzle #35

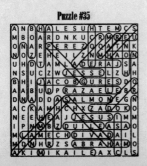

Puzzle #36

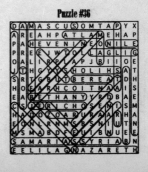

Puzzle #37

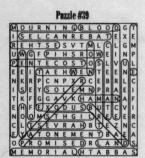

Puzzle #38

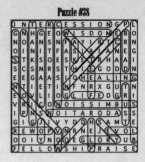

Puzzle #39

Puzzle #40

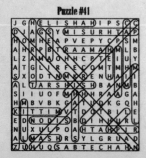

Puzzle #41

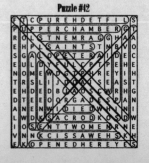

Puzzle #42

www.OneStrokeTV.com

JUMBO BIBLE WORD GAMES
VOLUMES 1 AND 2

www.christina Cooks

If you like
Bible-based
word games,
you'll love
these
books!

Featuring:
**Crosswords, Word Searches, Acrostics,
CryptoScriptures, Anagrams, Decodes,
Telephone Scrambles, and More!**

448 pages each, only $5.97

Available wherever
books are sold.
Or order from:

**Barbour Publishing, Inc.
P.O. Box 719
Uhrichsville, OH 44683**
http://www.barbourbooks.com

If you order by mail add $2.00 to your order for shipping.
Prices subject to change without notice.